START
Thinking

Where's My Shirt?

Sally Hewitt

QED Publishing

QED

First published in the UK in 2005 by
QED Publishing
A Quarto Group company
226 City Road
London EC1V 2TT
www.qed-publishing.co.uk

A Catalogue record for this book is available from the British Library.

ISBN 1 84538 155 6

Written by Sally Hewitt
Designed by Caroline Grimshaw
Editor Hannah Ray
Illustrated by Sue King

Series Consultant Anne Faundez
Publisher Steve Evans
Creative Director Louise Morley
Editorial Manager Jean Coppendale

Printed and bound in China

Cast List

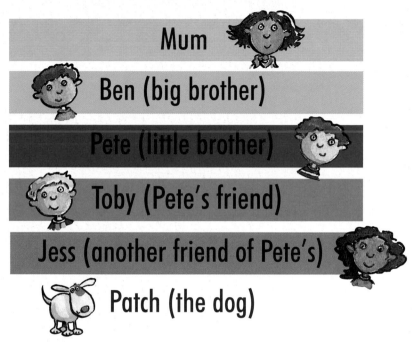

Mum

Ben (big brother)

Pete (little brother)

Toby (Pete's friend)

Jess (another friend of Pete's)

Patch (the dog)

Props

- Toy cars
- A wash basket
- A pair of socks and some other clothes
- A sports bag
- A towel
- A dog basket
- A shred of material
- Two football shirts (Toby wearing one)

Setting

The play takes place inside Pete and Ben's house.
To start, Pete, Toby and Jess are playing with some toy cars on the floor. Toby is wearing a football shirt. The wash basket, Ben's sports bag and the dog basket (containing the shred of material) are dotted around the stage.

Ben:	(*Shouting from off stage*) Mum! Where's my football shirt?
Mum:	(*Shouting from off stage*) In your wardrobe.
Ben:	(*Shouting from off stage*) It's not there! I've looked.
Pete:	(*Looking up from toys*) Oh no!
Toby, Jess:	What's the matter?

Ben: *(Shouting from off stage)* If anyone's taken it, I'll …

Toby: Did you take it, Pete?

Pete: I only borrowed it!

(Enter Ben.)

Ben: Where's my football shirt, Pete?

Pete: I don't know!

(Exit Ben.)

Toby:	You look worried, Pete.
Jess:	DO you know where Ben's shirt is?
Pete:	No, I don't. I did borrow Ben's shirt, but I don't remember where I put it.
Toby:	But you've got your own football shirt, just like mine!
Jess:	Yes. So why did you borrow Ben's shirt?
Pete:	Because I couldn't find mine.

Toby:	What will Ben do when he finds out that you've lost his shirt?
Jess:	He'll go crazy!
Toby:	What DID you do with it?
Jess:	Think hard, Pete.
Pete:	I AM thinking. Very hard!

Pete: I might have put it in the wash basket!

(They look in the wash basket and pull out clothes and a pair of socks.)

Toby: Pooh! Cheesy socks!

Pete: But no football shirt.

Mum: *(Shouting from off stage)* Have you looked in the wash basket, Ben?

Toby, Jess: Oh no!

(They bundle the clothes back into the basket. Enter Ben.)

Ben: (*Looking in wash basket*) It's not in the wash basket.

(*To Pete*) If you've had my football shirt ...

(*Exit Ben.*)

Toby, Jess: (*To audience*) Pete's in BIG trouble!

Pete: I might have put it back in Ben's sports bag.

Jess: Let's have a look.

(They look in Ben's sports bag and pull out a towel.)

Toby: Yuk! Soggy towel!

Pete: But no football shirt.

Mum: *(Shouting from off stage)* Have you looked in your sports bag?

Toby, Jess:	Oh no!
	(They bundle the towel back into the bag. Enter Ben.)
Ben:	What are you three up to?
All three	Nothing!
Ben:	Hmm!
	(Looking in sports bag) It's not here.
	(Exit Ben.)

Pete:	I remember!
Toby, Jess:	Good.
Pete:	(*Shaking head*) Bad!
	I put on the football shirt. I looked great.
Toby, Jess:	Yes?
Pete:	I went into the garden and I played football. I was brilliant!
Toby, Jess:	Yes?
Pete:	And then …
Toby, Jess:	Yes?
Pete:	I fell in the mud!
Toby, Jess:	Oh no!

Jess: So, what did you do with Ben's shirt?

Pete: I hid it in the dog's basket.

Toby: In Patch's basket?

Jess: What did you do that for?

Toby: Why didn't you tell your Mum?

Jess: Why didn't you tell Ben?

Pete: (*Wailing*) I was afraid they would be cross with me!

Toby: They'll be cross with you now!

Jess: Quick. Let's look in Patch's basket.

(*They look in the dog's basket.*)

Toby: It must be here somewhere.

Pete: (*Holding up shred of material*) Uh oh …

Toby: What's that?

Pete: I think it's Ben's football shirt.

Jess: What's happened to it?

Pete: (*Wailing*) Patch has eaten it!

(*Enter Ben. Takes the shred and holds it up.*)

Ben: What's this?

Pete: (*Shaking with fear*) It's your football shirt.

Ben: My football shirt?

Pete: Patch ate it.

Ben: What do you mean, "Patch ate it"?

Wait 'til I get my hands on you!

(*Pete, Toby and Jess run around the stage.*
Ben and Patch chase after them.)

(Enter Mum holding Ben's football shirt.)

Mum: Here it is!

All: *(Stopping running)* Here's what?

Mum: Ben's football shirt. It was in the washing machine with Patch's blanket. I can't think how it got there!

Ben: But I don't understand. If Mum's got my shirt, then what's this?

(Ben holds up scrap.)

Toby: Well, if it's not Ben's shirt …

Jess: and it's not Patch's blanket …

Toby, Jess: Then it must be …

Pete: *(Wailing)* My football shirt!

All: Oh, Patch!

What do you think?

If you borrow something from someone, what should you do?

Why did Pete borrow Ben's football shirt?

Why were
the wash bag
and Ben's
sports bag
good places
to look for
the shirt?

Can you remember
what Pete, Jess and
Toby found while
they were looking
for the shirt?

Can you remember, in order, what Pete did with Ben's shirt?

Why didn't Pete want to tell his Mum or Ben about getting the shirt dirty?

How do you
think Ben's shirt
got into the
washing machine?

What had happened
to Pete's shirt?

Parents' and teachers' notes

- Look at the cover of the book with your child and talk about the picture. What can your child see?
- Read the title and explain that the title is the name of the play. Read the author's name and explain that this is the person who wrote the play.
- Explain that a play is acted in front of an audience, but that it can also be fun simply to read a play aloud, with different people reading each part.
- Look at the cast list at the beginning of the play. Explain that the cast list is a list of all the characters who appear in the play.
- Together, discuss what each of the characters might look like and how their voices might sound.
- Explain that actors often wear costumes to make them look like the characters they are playing. Think about how the characters in this play could dress up. How could you make the actor who is playing Patch look like a dog?
- Explain that props are objects that actors use in a play. Find the list of props that are used in this play (see page 3).

- Talk about plays that your child might have seen at a theatre or at school.
- Find the stage directions in the play (*in italics*). Explain that these directions help the actors to know what to do.
- Together, pretend to be Pete saying "Oh no!" on page 4, and "I AM thinking. Very hard!" on page 7. Then pretend to be Toby saying "Pooh! Cheesy socks!" on page 8, and Ben saying "What's this?" on page 16. Think about the characters' actions, the look on their faces and the sound of their voices.
- Why are some of the words in the script in capital letters? Try reading some of the lines that feature words in capital letters. Firstly, read the lines emphasizing the words in capitals. Read the lines again, this time without the emphasis. Which sounds better?
- Talk about how Pete felt when he heard Ben asking his mum for his football shirt.
- Discuss who are the main characters in the play. What makes them the main characters?